GORGIAS REPRINT SERIES

Volume 24

Early Christianity Outside
The Roman Empire

Early Christianity outside the Roman Empire

Two Lectures delivered at Trinity College, Dublin, by F. CRAWFORD BURKITT, M.A., Trinity College, Cambridge.

GORGIAS PRESS
2002

First Gorgias Press Edition.

Copyright © 2002 by Gorgias Press LLC.

All rights reserved under International and Pan-American Copyright Conventions. Published in the United States of America by Gorgias Press LLC, New Jersey, from the original edition published by Cambridge University Press in 1899.

ISBN 1-931956-06-5

GORGIAS PRESS
46 Orris Ave., Piscataway, NJ 08854 USA
www.gorgiaspress.com

Printed in the United States of America

I dedicate this Book

to the Rev. GEORGE SALMON D.D.

Provost of Trinity College, Dublin,

in grateful acknowledgment

of his kindness to myself

and in admiration of the unfailing acuteness

of his critical judgment.

"*With matter of Heresie the West hath beene often and much troubled; but the East part neuer quiet, till the deluge of miserie wherein now they are, ouerwhelmed them. The chiefest cause whereof doth seeme to haue lien in the restlesse wits of the Grecians, euermore proud of their owne curious and subtile inuentions, which when at any time they had contriued, the great facilitie of their language serued them readily to make all things faire and plausible to men's vnderstanding. Those graund hereticall impieties therefore, which most highly and immediatly touched God and the glorious Trinitie, were all in a manner the monsters of the East.*"

HOOKER, *Ecclesiasticall Politie* v iii.

INTRODUCTION.

To the student of general history Christianity makes its appearance as a Greek religion. The first Christian communities of any considerable size had their home in the great Greek cities on the eastern shores of the Mediterranean. In Alexandria, in Antioch, in Ephesus, in Smyrna, in Corinth—all near the sea, and in easy communication with one another—the little Churches came into being and developed their organisation. The whole Ecclesiastical vocabulary is Greek. Bishops, Priests, Deacons, the Laity, Baptism, the Eucharist, all the terms are Greek in origin. It is the same with literature. From the alien religion out of which Christianity had sprung the Church inherited her Sacred Books in a Greek translation, and the writings of Christians that after a time were added on to the Canon of

Scripture as a New Volume—these writings were composed in Greek also. In a word, the Church grew up on Greek soil.

The life of the Greek cities reacted on the development of the Churches. The thought and activity of small and progressive bodies must always be largely determined by the atmosphere of the great world outside, whether by way of protest or of assimilation. For this reason early Christian literature, apart from the Jewish controversy, is mainly occupied with an attack upon Greek vices and the Greek Pantheon. With these no terms were possible. But as Christianity advanced an antagonist came on the scene more honourable and therefore more dangerous than Jupiter and his court or even than the Genius of the Emperor. No Religion could establish itself in the Greek-speaking world without coming to a reckoning with Greek Philosophy. Christianity had to face the old problems of the One and the Many, of Mind and Matter, of the infinite Divine Essence and its Manifestation in time and place.

Not that the Church, the main body of Christians, was in any hurry to engage in these difficult studies. They were forced on her from outside, from the borderland between Christianity and Heathendom, where thinkers such as Valentinus and Basilides attempted to unite the science and philosophy of the then civilised world with the life and doctrines of the new religion. The instinct of the Church, rather than her logical power, rejected the early Gnostics and their Ogdoads, but it was not possible to go on for ever with mere refutation. After three centuries a system was elaborated which the Church was able to recognise, and the Christian Faith was enshrined in a fixed symbol, which remains to this day as the accepted Christian account of the nature of God in Himself and of the relations between God and man. The Creeds mark the final Concordat between Christianity and Philosophy.

We all know that this is not the whole truth. The Church may have grown up on Greek soil, but Christianity itself is not Greek in origin.

The very earliest stage of all, that stage which it is most important for all of us to know and understand, is not Greek but Semitic. Our Lord was not sent save unto the lost sheep of the House of Israel. He lived the life of a Jew. He spoke in the current dialect of Palestine to His fellow-countrymen, and His conversations with his friends and His controversies with His foes turned on the things which troubled or interested the Jewish community of Palestine in the early part of the first century of our Era. Christ came not to promulgate a Creed, a form of words containing the quintessence of philosophical truth, but to live a life among men; and for us to feel the true force of His words, to appreciate the attitude He took up towards the current hopes and beliefs of those among whom He lived, we must find out and understand those beliefs. We must learn the language that His contemporaries spoke and study their phraseology.

When we attempt to do this we catch a glimpse of a very different world from that of Greek

Christianity. Alas, it is only a glimpse! The great catastrophe of the Jewish War, culminating with the sack of Jerusalem, finally separated the Church and the Synagogue. The Jewish state came to an end, and with it perished the primitive Semitic Christianity. The Christians of Judaea fled to the mountains, and when the troubles were over the survivors seem to have mingled themselves with the Greek-speaking urban population. Thus the one community which might have preserved the earliest traditions was swallowed up. So far as we can find out, Christianity ceased in the land of its birth, save that a small colony about which we only know the Greek names of its Bishops is said to have struggled on in Jerusalem. The shadow of their names falls across the page of Eusebius, but no deed or word is assigned to the silent figures.

Thus it has come to pass that our information even about the outward events of our Lord's ministry is so painfully scanty. The story of the earthly life of Jesus of Nazareth and of the first days of the infant community was known to the

Church, and has come down to us, only through certain literary channels. Those events of the early Galilean ministry which are recorded in S. Mark's narrative are known to us, but how few others! The Church's acquaintance with the first stage of Christianity rested on written documents, not on living tradition : for good and for evil the Greeks did not know Christ after the flesh.

Let me remind you in passing that this is not a mere literary question of *Quellenkritik*. On the contrary, it is the keystone of Protestantism. The one thing which historically justifies us in breaking with the Catholic tradition is this breach of continuity at the earliest period. We are entitled to criticise the Greek Gospels freely, to suggest on due evidence that phrases or figures have been wrongly or imperfectly apprehended, in a word we have a right privately to revise the judgments of the Church, mainly because the Church of the second century was so far removed in spirit and in knowledge from the life of Judaea in our Lord's day. Do not let me be misunderstood. I am not maintaining that this separation was not inevitable. The work of the Church was to overcome the world, not to furnish material for archaeologists. Still, if we could know more about the beliefs, the rites, the sacraments, of the community of ' Nazarenes ' that S. Jerome mentions more than once with such tantalising brevity, it is my firm conviction that we should possess a key that would unlock many of the riddles which obstruct the Evangelic history and darken to us the recorded sayings of Christ.

But if between the Church of the second century and the Apostles there is a great gulf fixed, in what words are we to describe the difference between the Nicene and Post-Nicene Church and primitive Christianity ? Here all will acknowledge the vastness of the change. At the same time, it may be said that the change was due to natural growth : the line that it took was, as a matter of fact, the historical development of Christianity. The Church of Justin Martyr and Irenaeus is undoubtedly continuous with that of Athanasius and Hilary, and that Church came to Nicaea and proceeded to Chalcedon. After all, the Creeds are merely the formal ratification of the best theology of the great Churchmen. The new Constitution was, in fact, inevitable—like the promulgation of the Pope's Infallibility at a later day, long after the dogma had been a pious inference in the Roman communion.

This may indeed be so, and I for one should be very willing to believe that the rigidity of the later Church was indispensable for it to withstand the shock of the Barbarian invasions which swept away the ancient Civilisation. But the object that I have chiefly had in view in these Lectures is to glance at a strangely neglected branch of the Church, a branch in full communion and fellowship with the rest of the Christian body and proud of its Apostolic descent, yet cut off by political and linguistic circumstances from that struggle with Greek philosophy which so greatly influenced the Christianity of the Greek-speaking populations within the Roman Empire.

I speak, of course, of the Christianity of the Euphrates valley, of the Church whose language was Syriac and its metropolis Edessa. But before we settle down to our study of this Church we shall do well to consider how it came to pass that it is the only historical rival of the Greeks.

Let us look round the Roman Empire. To the north and west it is obvious that Greek-speaking Christianity could have no competitors. Marcion of Pontus to all intents and purposes counts as a Greek. The few Christians of Armenia used Syriac until the 4th century. The Latin Christianity of the West and of N. Africa is wholly the child of Greek Christianity. At a much later period it also developed distinctive characteristics, but it inherited nothing of primitive Christianity which it did not get through Greek Christianity. The language, the laws, the customs of the Latins are all utterly foreign to Palestine and Semitic thought.

Nor does Egypt supply anything for our purpose. Christianity was early established in Alexandria, but Alexandria was less Egyptian than Gibraltar is

Spanish. There is little to shew that Christianity spread among the native Egyptians till the rise of monasticism, still less that a Christian literature existed in any Coptic dialect before the latter half of the 3rd century. The vast increase of information about the condition of Egypt under the Empire which the last fifty years has witnessed, has served only to confirm the familiar words of Gibbon. " The progress of Christianity was for a long time confined within the limits of a single city, which was itself a foreign colony ; and, till the close of the 2nd century, the predecessors of Demetrius were the only prelates of the Christian Church....The body of the natives, a people distinguished by a sullen inflexibility of temper, entertained the new doctrine with coldness and reluctance ; and even in the time of Origen it was rare to meet with an Egyptian who had surmounted his early prejudices in favour of the sacred animals of his country. As soon, indeed, as Christianity ascended the throne, the zeal of those barbarians obeyed the prevailing impulsion ; the cities of Egypt were filled with bishops, and the deserts of Thebais swarmed with hermits[1]."

The political fortunes of Edessa, the metropolis of the Syriac-speaking Church, offer a remarkable contrast to any other centre of early Christianity. Until A.D. 216, in the reign of Caracalla, Edessa was outside the Roman Empire. The Toparch or kinglet of the place, whose name seems always to have been Abgar or Ma'nu, owed some allegiance to the Parthian monarchs, but the little state enjoyed most of the conditions favourable for independent literary development. The language of the people was also the language of the nobles and of government. The local patriotism was that of the ancient Greek states or the Italian commonwealths of a later day, and was as far as possible removed from the cosmopolitanism of the Empire. At the same time the city was not cut off from a wide intercourse with surrounding communities. The Aramaic of Edessa was more than a mere local dialect : it was the medium of commerce throughout the

[1] Bury's *Gibbon* ii 60.

Euphrates valley, while the Aramaic of Palmyra and of Palestine hardly differed from it more than Lowland 'Scots' differs from the standard English. Edessa, in one word, was situated on the confines of two great civilisations, the Greek and the Persian, while at the same time it had not been robbed of its own Semitic culture. The extant remains of Syriac literature are almost wholly the product of later ages and less fortunate conditions; it is the misfortune of Edessa, not her fault, that she was unable to maintain her intellectual freedom through the shock of the Persian wars. But the ease and vigour of the earliest surviving literature of the Syriac-speaking Church, whether prose, poetry, or philosophical discussion, unmistakably reflect the glory of Edessa's three hundred years of honourable independence.

Christianity appears to have reached the Euphrates valley about the middle of the second century. The Bishops of Edessa trace their succession to Serapion, Bishop of Antioch from 190 to 203, and there is all the more reason for believing this tradition to be historically exact, because it contradicts so glaringly the alternative story of the successful preaching of Christianity at Edessa by Addai, one of the 72 disciples. We need not, however, delay long over the outward history of the Syriac-speaking Church. The subject has been well worked out by the Rev. Prof. Tixeront, a French scholar of the school of Duchesne[1]. The main thing that concerns us here is that Christianity was planted in Edessa and the Church organisation established there while it was yet an independent state.

For the inner character of Syriac-speaking Christianity in its early stages we must turn from history to the surviving documents. The list, alas, is miserably scanty. The later Syrians had different tastes and a different standard of orthodoxy from their forefathers and we may certainly add from ourselves. Syriac literature, as it has come down to us, consists for the most part of the contents of

[1] *Les Origines de l'Église d'Édesse*...par L.-J. Tixeront, Paris, 1888.

one great Monophysite library, that of the Convent of S. Mary Deipara in the Nitrian desert. The mere fact that it did not contain a MS. of the *Diatessaron* is enough to shew that its collection of the earlier Syriac writings is quite inadequate. Nevertheless, enough remains to give us some idea of the temper of the first two centuries of Syriac Christianity in its very varied forms.

It will be convenient to give here a list of the works which supply the materials for our investigation. They may be grouped under six heads, as follows :

1.   The Old Testament in Syriac, commonly called the *Pĕshittâ*.

2.   The *Evangeliòn da-Mĕpharrĕshê* or Old Syriac Version of the Gospels, and the closely allied *Diatessaron* of Tatian.

3.   The *Doctrine of Addai* and the early Martyrologies (*Acts of Sharbêl, Barsamyâ*, etc.).

4.   The *Book of the Laws of Countries*, commonly known as 'Bardesanes *De Fato*,' but really composed by Bardaisan's disciple Philip.

5. The Syriac *Acts of Thomas*, including the great Gnostic *Hymn* which is ascribed by modern scholars to Bardaisan himself.

6. The *Homilies* of Aphraates.

It is the two last of these, the *Acts of Thomas* and Aphraates' *Homilies*, which more especially concern us. You will notice that I have included neither the works of Ephraim Syrus nor the revised version of the N.T. in Syriac which goes by the name of the Peshitta. The reason is only partly chronological. Ephraim's chief literary activity and the publication of the N.T. Peshitta may both be placed about the middle of the 4th century. But they stand apart from the list given above for other reasons. Both represent that effort to keep pace with the Greeks, which ossified the Syriac language and landed the Syriac-speaking Churches in the course of a hundred years in the opposite errors of the Monophysites and the Nestorians.

The N.T. Peshitta is a revision of the Old Syriac, not a fresh translation. It must have been the work of learned and conscientious scholars : its great merit is that it left so much of the old work standing. Accuracy and timidity are the chief characteristics of the revisers, and we can still trace the influence of Greek theology and the Greek grammarians as well as the use of Greek MSS.[1]

Ephraim's excessive verbosity makes it difficult to discover his real theological position. In a time of transition, such as he lived in, the art of saying nothing in a great many words must have been exceedingly useful, and the saint who preferred to glue together the pages of Apollinaris's book rather than attempt to confute the writer must have been aware that argument was not his strong point. The ultimate reasons which led to the short-lived and disastrous triumph of Greek thought over the native Syriac Christianity were political rather than theological, and Ephraim only too well represents the temporary and verbal complaisance of the Syriac-

---

[1] The *Word* and the *Spirit* are treated for theological purposes as masculine, contrary to the genius of the language, and in Joh i 14 *flesh* is substituted for the Old Syriac *body*. In Grammar we may notice the consistent omission of the Semitic 'and' at the beginning of the apodosis, *e.g.* in Lk xii 46.

speaking subjects of the Christianised Empire at the end of the 4th century[1]. It was a state of things which could not last long, and in a couple of generations after Ephraim hardly a single orthodox community was left in Mesopotamia. Let us not linger now over the ill-matched union of Greek and Semitic thought, but go back to the time when the Syriac-speaking Church was still free and innocent.

The Old Testament in Syriac first claims our attention, and chiefly because it may serve to remind us of one most important factor among the populations of the Euphrates valley, *viz.* the Jews. The appellation *Pĕshiṭtâ* (*i.e.* 'simple') by which this version is familiarly known to us does not seem to be older than the 9th century. It was probably given to distinguish it from the work of Paul of Tella, which is a translation made from Origen's *Hexapla* and consequently embellished with a

[1] Ephraim's emancipation from the native tradition is well illustrated by the fact that he quotes the Apocalypse by name (*Opp. Syr.* ii 332 c), though the book was not, and is not to this day, included in the Syriac Canon.

complicated apparatus of critical signs. But the
Syriac Vulgate of the O.T. is much more ancient
than the name *Pĕshiṭtâ*. It is largely and accurately quoted by Aphraates, and unmistakeable
traces of its use appear in the *Acts of Thomas* : in
other words, it has as early an attestation as our
surviving materials carry us.

The Peshitta is a direct translation from the
Hebrew, in all essentials from the Massoretic text.
Some books, such as Chronicles, are amazingly
paraphrased, but the variations appear to be due to
the caprice of the translator or his exegetical
tradition, not to differences of reading in the under-
lying Hebrew. Apart from intentional paraphrase
the translation is fairly done : so well, in fact, that
we cannot think of it as the work of Gentiles. It
seems to me not improbable that it is a monument
of Jewish learning of the great age of translations,
the age of Aquila and Symmachus, which has been
taken over by the Christian Church. Had it been
wholly the work of Christians, I cannot but think
that we should have heard of the singular erudition

of the translators and of their courage in breaking away from the Greek tradition. However that may be, the Peshitta is in itself an unanswerable demonstration that the earliest Syriac Church contained a large Jewish element. This is quite in accordance with the early traditions in the *Doctrine of Addai*[1], and harmonises (as we shall see) with what is found in Aphraates. Thus the independent civilisation of Edessa made a vernacular translation necessary, while the presence of an influential Jewish factor in the infant Church secured that the translation of the Old Testament should be made from the original Hebrew.

The earliest N.T. Canon of the Syriac-speaking Church consisted of the Gospel, the Epistles of S. Paul, and the Acts. "The Law and the Prophets and the Gospel from which ye read every day before the people, and the Epistles of Paul which Simon Cephas sent us from the city of Rome, and the Acts of the Twelve Apostles which

---

[1] *Phillips*, E. tr. pp. 32, 33.

John the son of Zebedee sent us from Ephesus,—
from these writings shall ye read in the Churches of
the Messiah and besides them nothing else shall ye
read." This is the Canon of the *Doctrine of
Addai*[1], and the list is confirmed by the actual
practice of Aphraates. I am not going to enter on
the difficult and disputed question of the relative
priority of the translation into Syriac of the Four
Gospels and of the *Diatessaron*, important as it is in
many ways. The investigation would involve us in
a mass of detail quite foreign to the scale of this
Lecture. Speaking generally, we may say that the
scanty notices in Syriac writings and the usage of
Aphraates himself are most naturally interpreted if
we assume the *Diatessaron* to have been first in the
field. Before the discovery of the Sinai Palimpsest
of the Four Gospels in the Old Syriac version
there was no doubt that the arguments for the
priority of the *Diatessaron* seemed much the stronger.
But now the balance of internal evidence has very
considerably shifted : the more intimately we know

[1] Syriac text, p. 46.

the *Evangeliôn da-Mĕpharrĕshê*, the more primitive seems to have been its original form.

What concerns us now is not so much the literary history of the Gospel in Syriac as the light thrown by these early versions on the knowledge accessible to the translators. The earliest retranslation of our Lord's words into a Semitic tongue cannot fail to contain much that is of interest for us. And we find, as might have been anticipated, a mixture of happy intuition and of helplessness. At every turn we are reminded that we are dealing with mere translations and adaptations of the Greek Gospels, yet with translations which have often the rare opportunity of being more exact and more happy than the original work. Happily also the translator was unhampered by pedantic methods, such as some four centuries later disfigured the effort of Justinian's clergy to give the people of Palestine the Scriptures in their own tongue: no version is more idiomatic than the Old Syriac or less affected. The Proper Names are given in the original forms or an approximation thereto: *Ḥalpai*,

Mattai and *Malku* replace Αλφαῖος, Μαθθαῖος and Μάλχος. By the Latins and ourselves Χριστὸς is transliterated, but the Syriac has *Mĕshîḥâ*, the Messiah or Anointed one; in the accusation of Lk xxiii 2 ("saying that he is Christ a king") the term used is *Malkâ Mĕshîḥâ*, the very same phrase syllable for syllable that we so often meet with in Jewish literature and usually translate by 'King Messiah[1].' It is still more surprising and instructive to find that 'salvation' is identified by the Syriac usage with 'life.' Σωτὴρ is *Maḥyânâ* 'Life-giver,' and 'to be saved' is 'to live.' This is the more remarkable, as Syriac has several words meaning 'to deliver,' 'to protect,' and 'to be safe and sound.' May we not therefore believe that this identification of 'salvation' and 'life' is the genuine Aramaic usage, and that the Greek Gospels have in this instance introduced a distinction which was not made by Christ and His Aramaic-speaking disciples?

---

[1] According to Dalman (*Worte Jesu*, 240) we ought not to render it '*King Messiah*' but ' *The anointed King.*'

But exegetical help of this kind is not always to be got out of the Syriac versions. In cases of real difficulty we can often see that the translator is only struggling with the unknown meaning of the Greek, and that his rendering, for all its Semitic appearance, contains no element of originality. There is one very marked instance, which will serve to illustrate what I mean. No phrase in the Gospel is more characteristic or more obscure than the title ὁ υἱὸς τοῦ ἀνθρώπου, *the Son of Man*, used by our Lord of Himself in many very varied aspects of His mission. To seize the full meaning, or meanings, we must be able to retranslate the Greek words into the original Aramaic expression. It is well known that in some circumstances the Aramaic dialects use the phrase 'a son of man' for 'a human being'; moreover, there is an undoubted connexion of some kind between our Lord's use of 'The Son of Man' and the very similar phrase in Daniel's Vision[1] which itself was written in Aramaic. For many reasons, therefore, we turn to the Syriac

[1] Dan vii 13.

renderings of ὁ υἱὸς τοῦ ἀνθρώπου with some justi-
fiable expectation of obtaining help. As a matter
of fact, we get none at all. The ordinary rendering
in the Old Syriac documents, as in the Peshitta
N.T., is *b'reh d''nâshâ*—a phrase sufficiently like
barnashâ 'a human being' to sound original, but
really just as little native Syriac as 'The Son of
Man' is English. 'The Son of Man' has no
natural meaning in English : it is a mere con-
ventional rendering of ὁ υἱὸς τοῦ ἀνθρώπου.
Similarly, *b'reh d''nâshâ* has no natural meaning in
Syriac. Moreover, it is not the rendering of the
O.T. Peshitta in Dan vii 13, which has *bar
'nâshîn* which means (if it has any real meaning)
'son of some folk.' Nor is this all. *B'reh d''nâshâ*,
if not a very illuminating translation, is at least
inoffensive. But the earliest Syriac documents
give us here and there, sometimes singly and sometimes in conjunction, the amazing alternative *b'reh
d''γαβρâ.* This is a literal, a too literal, rendering
of ὁ υἱὸς τοῦ ἀνθρώπου. It means *filius uiri*, 'the
on of the man.' The fact that so inadequate a

rendering is actually found can only be explained on the supposition that it was the primitive Syriac equivalent for the Greek words. But if it could be tolerated at all, there must have been an utter absence of exegetical tradition in the Church.

Thus we come back to the point from which we started. The Greek-speaking Church and its daughters were wholly dependent for its historical information about our Lord and His times on the bare letter of the Greek Gospels, and the only advantage in this respect enjoyed by the Christians of Edessa was that their native idiom was akin to that of Palestine.

In studying the Syriac-speaking branch of the Church, therefore, we may not hope to find an organisation more primitive than that of Justin Martyr or Hegesippus. But we know too little about the Church of the second century not to be grateful for anything that promises to throw light upon its aims and beliefs. And here the Syriac evidence is of real value. The Christianity planted in the Euphrates valley in the latter half of the second century seems to have developed more slowly —in other words, changed less—than that of the Greeks. Two hundred years later, in the middle of the fourth century, we still hear the old watchwords in their full vigour from the mouth of a monk and bishop of the orthodox communion.

THE CREED OF
APHRAATES.

To appreciate the significance of the *Homilies* of Aphraates we must first consider their date and the personality of the writer.   About the date there is fortunately no doubt.   Of the twenty-two Homilies the first ten were composed A.D. 337, and the remaining twelve A.D. 344 : the additional Homily *On the Cluster* is dated A.D. 345.   Thus they appeared in the stormy years between the death of Constantine and the second return of S. Athanasius from exile.   The author, Aphraates (or more accurately Afrahaṭ), obtained from his countrymen the name of the Persian Sage.   He was a monk, and must also have been a bishop.   Dr William Wright conjectures that he was bishop of the

Convent of S. Matthew near Mosul [1]. It is certain that he had a seat in a Synod, held A.D. 344 in the diocese of Seleucia and Ctesiphon, and that he was selected to draw up the encyclical letter of the Synod. This letter he subsequently published as No. 14 of the Homilies.

Thus Aphraates was one of the foremost leaders of the orthodox Syriac-speaking Church in the second quarter of the 4th century. Some of his fellow-bishops had been to Nicaea, and he himself is writing in the very middle of the great Arian controversy. His words, therefore, cannot fail to shew the temper of his time. Moreover, the plan of his great work is admirably fitted to give us the information we are seeking. We speak of the 'Homilies' of Aphraates, but the volume of discourses which goes by that name is not a collection

---

[1] Wright's *Syriac Literature*, p. 33, following a statement in a late MS. (B. M. *Orient.* 1017). A full discussion of the rank and status of Aphraates is to be found on pp. 157, 158 of Dr Gwynn's *Introduction* to the translations of select works of Aphraates and Ephraim in vol. xiii of the *Select Library of Nicene and post-Nicene Fathers.*

of occasional sermons. On the contrary, it is a complete and ordered exposition of the Christian Faith in answer to a request for information from an inquirer. The twenty-two Homilies correspond to the twenty-two letters of the Semitic Alphabet, and the first word of each Homily begins with the corresponding letter of the Alphabet in order, the first with *Alaph*, the second with *Beth*, and so right through. This is not a mere fanciful quip, but a serious plan to enable the true order of the discourses to be ascertained and, if needful, restored. It is difficult to interpolate or mutilate an acrostic without immediate · discovery[1]. And as if the acrostic arrangement were not enough, Aphraates enumerates the series in order at the end of the twenty-second Homily.

Once more I must remind you of the state of Ecclesiastical affairs at the date of the publication of Aphraates' works. The Council of Nicaea has

---

[1] The acrostic arrangement has actually enabled Wright to dispose at once of N. Antonelli's argument about the 14th Homily (Wright's *Aphraates*, p. 9 note).

been held not half a generation ago, the Emperor
Constantine has just died, and Athanasius is in exile.
The flames of the Arian controversy are consuming
the vitals of the Empire.   Christianity is divided up
into rival camps, each anathematising the other,
while according to one authority the public posting
system is quite thrown out of gear by the troops of
eager bishops hastening from synod to synod[1].
What then has Aphraates to say about the crisis in
the Church ?

The astonishing answer is—*absolutely nothing*.
Neither Athanasius nor Arius is even mentioned.
We hear nothing of Homoousians or Homœousians,
Semiarians or Sabellians.   Incidentally Aphraates
names ' *Marcion*, who doth not acknowledge our
Creator to be good ' ; he speaks of ' *Valentinus*, who
preacheth that his Creators are many, and that God
in His perfection hath not been uttered by the
mouth, neither hath the understanding searched
Him out ' ; and he devotes a sentence of con-
temptuous reprobation to the Babylonian arts of the

[1] *Ammianus Marcellinus* xxi 16, quoted by Gibbon ii 359.

Manichees[1]. But upon the controversies of his own day he is silent. This does not come from enmity to the Greeks, for in Homily V (*Of the Wars*) he expresses at length his firm conviction, based upon the visions of Daniel, of the ultimate failure of the Persian attack upon the Empire[2]. Nor does it come from want of interest in theological discussion, as we may see from the very title of Homily XVII '*Of the Messiah, that He is the Son of God.*' To this Homily we shall return presently, but we shall best do justice to Aphraates by starting in the order he has so carefully indicated. Instead of picking out the most definite or startling doctrinal passages, let us begin with Homily I *On Faith*[3]. Out of the abundance of the heart the mouth speaketh : in a doctrinal treatise that which is put first must in the eyes of the author be fundamental.

Faith, then, according to Aphraates, is like a building made of various materials of various colours.

---

[1] *Aphr.* III 9.   [2] *Aphr.* v 6, 19, 24.
[3] This Homily is translated in full by Dr Gwynn, pp. 345—352. It has also been translated by Dr Budge in his edition of Philoxenus, vol. ii, pp. clxxv—clxxxvii.

But the foundation of our faith is Jesus Christ, the Rock upon which the whole is built, as said the prophets (§ 2). First a man believes, then loves, then hopes, then is justified and perfected, and he becomes a Temple for the Messiah to dwell in, as Jeremiah said : *The Temple of the LORD, the Temple of the LORD—ye are the Temple of the LORD, if ye will make fair your ways and your works* [1], and as said our Lord Himself *Ye are in Me, and I am in you* (§ 3). The man who has Faith will study to make himself worthy of being a dwelling-place of the Spirit of the Messiah. There must be Fasting, Prayer, Love, Alms, Humility, Virginity, Continence, Wisdom, Hospitality, Simplicity, Patience, Gentleness, Sadness [2], Purity : Faith asks for all these ornaments (§ 4). Christ is both the foundation and the inhabitant of the House of Faith : Jeremiah says men are the Temples of God and the Apostle said *The Spirit of Christ dwelleth in you.* This comes to the same thing, for the Lord said :

---

[1] Jer vii 4, 5 (*Pesh*).
[2] The technical term for the monastic life.

I and My Father are one (§ 5). The Messiah is spoken of by the prophets as a Stone or Rock (§§ 6—9), and as a Light (§§ 10, 11). He is the only foundation that can stand the fire (§§ 12, 13). Such Faith the Saints of old time had (§§ 14—16), and those also who were benefited by our Lord on earth (§ 17). Faith carries us up to heaven, saves us from the Deluge, looses the prisoners, quenches the fire, feeds the hungry, brings back from the grave, stops the mouths of lions, humbles the proud, and exalts the meek (§ 18).

Perhaps you may find this vague and rhetorical. But Aphraates does not leave us here. After the praise of Faith he goes on to tell us exactly in what it consists, and this Creed of his is so remarkable a document that I give it in full.

"For this," he says (§ 19), "is Faith :—

When a man shall believe in God, the Lord of all,
  That made the heaven and the earth and the seas
    and all that in them is,
  Who made Adam in His image,
  Who gave the Law to Moses,
  Who sent of His Spirit in the Prophets,
  Who sent moreover His Messiah into the world.

And that a man should believe in the coming to life of
    the dead,
And believe also in the mystery of Baptism:
    This is the Faith of the Church of God.
And that a man should separate himself
    from observing hours and sabbaths and months and
        seasons,
    and enchantments and divinations and Chaldaism and
        magic,
    and from fornication and from revelling and from vain
        doctrines, the weapons of the Evil One, and from
        the blandishment of honeyed words, and from
        blasphemy and from adultery,
And that no man should bear false witness,
and that none should speak with double tongues:
    These are the works of the Faith that is laid on the
        true Rock,
        which is the Messiah,
        upon Whom all the building doth rise."

You will recognise at once the spirit of this
Creed. It is familiar to us all; it has been familiar
to us for nearly twenty years, for it is the spirit
which pervades the *Didache*. To Aphraates
Christianity was the revelation of a Divine Spirit
dwelling in man and fighting against moral evil,
not first and foremost a tissue of philosophical
speculation about the nature of the Divinity in

itself. But this is wholly alien to the temper of Greek and Latin Christianity, as it manifests itself from the fourth century onward. According to the Creeds which to this day we recite, the inter-relation of the Trinity and the events of the Passion constitute the faith of the Church. Nor is this view confined to formal ecclesiastical documents.

> " Firmly I believe and truly
>   God is Three, and God is One;
> And I next acknowledge duly
>   Manhood taken by the Son."

So runs the beginning of Gerontius' dying confession in J. H. Newman's poem, and it only expresses in modern verse what the Church of the Empire would have us confess as the essence of the Christian Religion[1].

Not that Aphraates did not acknowledge the

---

[1] For a contrast to Aphraates in Syriac literature see Philoxenus, *Discourse* II 32 (Budge's Eng. Tr., p. 29). There are, it should be noticed, traces of a (baptismal) *Symbol* in Aphraates, *e.g.* "He is the First-born Son, the offspring of Mary...He suffered, lived again, ascended into the height...He is the Judge of dead and living, who shall sit on the Throne" (XIV 39).

Trinity, or was anything like a modern Unitarian.
The Syriac-speaking Church, in common with the
rest of Christendom, baptized in the Triple Name,
as is commanded in Matt xxviii 19. "The Head of
the man," says Aphraates (XXIII 63 = *Wright* 500),
"is the Messiah. O thou that swearest by thy head
and that falsely, if thou dost truly hold the three
great and glorious Names that were invoked upon
thy head, the Father and the Son and the Holy
Spirit, when thou didst receive the Seal of thy life,
—do not swear by thy head!" Or again (XXIII
60 = *Wright* 496): "Above the heavens, what is
there—who doth suffice to tell? Beneath the
earth, what is laid?—there is none to say! The
firmament—upon what is it stretched out, or the
heavens—upon what are they hung? The earth—
on what is it pillowed, or the deep—in what is it
fixed? We are of Adam, and here with our senses
we perceive little. Only this we know: that God
is one, and His Messiah one, and one the Spirit,
and one the Faith, and one Baptism. More than
thus far it doth not help us to speak; and if we

say more we fall short, and if we investigate we are helpless." After revolving round the theological circle, we are surprised to find that Gibbon ends where Aphraates had begun; "the incomprehensible mystery which excites our adoration eludes our enquiry[1]." It would have been well for the peace of the Christian world if it had always imitated the modesty of the Persian Sage.

One more point remains to be noticed in connexion with Aphraates' doctrine of the Trinity. In Semitic languages there is no neuter, and *Rûḥ*, the word for wind or spirit, is feminine; in the older Syriac literature, therefore, before the influence of Greek theology made itself felt, the Holy Spirit also is feminine. Thus in the Old Syriac version of Joh xiv 26 we actually read *The Spirit, the Paraclete, she shall teach you everything[2]*. And so it is only in accordance with the earliest usage that

---

[1] *Gibbon* ii 347.

[2] In the Peshitta *she* (or *it*) is changed to *he*. Another instance where the feminine usage seemed too heterodox to stand is Lk xii 12. But in many passages the feminine is retained even in the Peshitta, *e.g.* Lk iv 1, Joh vii 39.

in a doxology (XXIII 63 = *Wright* 498) Aphraates
ascribes, "glory and honour to the Father and to
His Son and to His Spirit, the living and holy,"
where *living* and *holy* are feminine adjectives in the
better MS. But he goes further : it is not a question
of mere grammatical niceties. In the treatise, *On
Virginity against the Jews* (XVIII 10 = *Wright* 354),
he says : "We have heard from the law that a man
will leave his father and his mother and will cleave
to his wife, and they will be one flesh ; and truly a
prophecy great and excellent is this. What father
and mother doth he forsake that taketh a wife ?
This is the meaning : that when a man not yet
hath taken a wife, he loveth and honoureth God his
Father, and the Holy Spirit his Mother, and he
hath no other love. But when a man taketh a
wife he forsaketh his Father and his Mother, those
namely that are signified above, and his mind is
united with this world ; and his mind and his heart
and his thought is dragged away from God into the
midst of the world, and he loveth and cherisheth it,
as a man loveth the wife of his youth, and the love

of her is different from that of his Father and of his Mother."

We shall find still more startling developments of this doctrine of the Spirit when we come to the Bardesanian *Acts of Thomas.* Here I would only remind you that there is very early Christian authority for it. In the ancient *Gospel according to the Hebrews,* as quoted by Origen and S. Jerome, our Lord Himself speaks of His Mother the Holy Spirit[1]. And before we condemn the doctrine altogether, let us remember that the age which followed its final disappearance polluted the Christian vocabulary with the word Θεοτόκος.

I should like also to point out that just as Aphraates' doctrine of the Spirit, strange as it appears to us, is only a survival of one of the most

---

[1] The authorities for this well-known saying are to be found *e.g.* in Westcott's *Introduction to the Study of the Gospels,* App. D. Origen (*in Joann.* II 12) explains it away by saying that the Holy Spirit does the will of the Father and therefore may rightly be described as the Mother of Christ, in accordance with Matt xii 50.

In Ephraim Syrus the Holy Spirit is still grammatically feminine, but no specially feminine functions are ascribed to primitive Christian beliefs, so too Homily XVII *Of the Messiah that He is the Son of God* is an echo of one of the most remarkable sayings recorded in S. John's Gospel[1]. The Homily, like so many that Aphraates wrote, is directed against the Jews, who complained that Christians worshipped a man whom they called Son of God, in defiance of God's own word *I am God, and there is none beside me*[2] (§ 1).

Her. "The Father *nods* and the Son *knows*; The works by the Spirit *are performed*." Beyond such generalities Ephraim does not go.

"Confess that the Father is;	Do not confess that He can be defined.
Believe that the Son hath been;	Do not believe that He can be searched out.
Affirm that the Holy Spirit is;	Do not affirm that She can be examined.
That they are One believe and affirm;	And that They are Three do not doubt.
Believe that the Father is first;	Affirm that the Son is second;
That the Holy Spirit also is—	Do not doubt She is the third."

(Ephr. *Opp. Syr.* iii 194: the change of tense in the second line may be due to the exigencies of metre). The chief point insisted on by Ephraim appears to be the *impalpability* of the Spirit (*e.g.* iii 161).

[1] Joh x 33—36. This Homily is translated in full by Dr Gwynn, pp. 387—392.

[2] Cf. Deut xxxii 39.

Aphraates sets himself the task of defending the Christian practice, even if he should concede to the Jews that Jesus whom the Christians call God was only a man. " Though," he continues, "we truly hold that Jesus our Lord is God the Son of God, and the King the Son of the King, Light from Light, Son[1] and Counsellor and Guide and Way and Saviour and Shepherd and Gatherer and Door and Pearl and Lamp; and by many Names is He called. But now we will shew that He is the Son of God and that He is God who from God hath come " (§ 2). For the name of divinity has been given to just men, as for instance to Moses, who was made a God not to Pharaoh only but also to Aaron[2] (§ 3), and though the Jews say God has no son, yet He called Israel His First-born[3], and Solomon His son[4]. David also says of them : *I have said, Ye are Gods and sons of the Highest all of you*[5]

---

[1] *Sic:* cf. Isaiah ix 6 and also § 9.

[2] Exod vi 1, vii 1.   [3] Exod iv 22, 23.

[4] 2 Sam vii 14; cf. Heb i 5.

[5] Ps lxxxii (lxxxi) 6.

(§4). God gives the most exalted titles to whom He will: He called impious Nebuchadnezzar *King of Kings*. For man was formed by Him in His own image to be a Temple for Him to dwell in, and therefore He gives to man honours which He denies to the Sun and the Moon and the host of Heaven[1] (§§ 5, 6). Man of all creatures was first conceived in God's mind[2], though he was not placed in the world till it was ready for him (§ 7). Why should not we worship Jesus, through whom we know God, Jesus who turned away our mind from vain superstitions and taught us to adore the One God, our Father and Maker, and to serve Him? Is it not better to do this than to worship the kings and emperors of this world, who not only are apostates themselves but drive others also to apostasy? (§ 8). Our Messiah has been spoken of in the prophets even to the details of the Crucifixion[3]

---

[1] Deut iv 17.   [2] Ps xc (lxxxix) 1, 2.

[3] Among other more ordinary *Testimonia* Aphraates quotes Zech xiv 6 (*In that day there shall be cold and frost*) as a prophecy of the cold day when Peter had to warm himself by the fire (Joh xviii 18).

(§§ 9, 10). We therefore will continue to worship before the Majesty of His Father, who has turned our worship unto Him. We call Him God, like Moses ; First-born and Son, like Israel ; Jesus, like Joshua the son of Nun ; Priest, like Aaron ; King, like David ; the great Prophet, like all the prophets; Shepherd, like the shepherds who tended and ruled Israel. And us, adds Aphraates, has he called Sons and made us His Brothers, and we have become His Friends (§§ 11, 12).

Nothing less than the full abstract here given does justice to Aphraates' style and method. It is surely most surprising and instructive to meet with work animated by this spirit in the middle of the 4th century. For my own part, I feel it follows too closely the lines of our Lord's answer to the Jews for me to venture to brand it as unorthodox.

In the following chapter we shall glance at the teaching of Aphraates upon Baptism, Marriage, and Asceticism : this will lead us on to the Gnostic doctrines found in the *Acts of Thomas*. But before leaving this part of the work let me once more call

attention to the absence of the Greek influence in
Aphraates. The Persian Sage lived outside the
Roman Empire and was educated in a culture but
little touched by Greek philosophy. He did not
feel that necessity for logical subordination, for the
due relation of the parts to the whole, which the
Greeks were the first of mankind to strive after.

And dare we say that he and his Church were
altogether to be pitied? It is unlikely that the
human intellect can form a logical system of the
Universe: a logical Creed or 'Weltanschauung' by
its very nature betrays its human parentage and
temporary value. With a most imperfect knowledge of the constitution of the world we live in, by
an uncritical use of Scripture, at a time when every
art and every science was decaying, the Greeks
attempted in a form of words to define the Inde-
finable. They succeeded for a while in obtaining
the allegiance of the Oriental Church, the time of
their victory being approximately the reigns of the
heathen Julian and the Arian Valens. Under
stress of persecution the Christians closed their

ranks and unified their public confession of Faith[1]. But what I have brought before you to-day from the works of Aphraates shews clearly that there was no inner unity between East and West. In the East the theology of S. Athanasius and S. Basil was a foreign graft, not a genuine natural growth : it is therefore not surprising that the Syriac-speaking Church broke away hardly a single generation after an orthodox Emperor was seated on the throne. The mass of the Orientals, especially those more distant from Constantinople and Antioch, became Nestorian ; and those who remained soon found that their position also was untenable. It was impossible for the barbarians to remain at peace with the Greeks : the Church was divided, and the way paved for the triumph of Islam.

[1] See Hort's *Two Dissertations*, pp. 128—133.

THE SACRAMENTS IN APHRAATES.

THE teaching of Aphraates about the Sacraments throws most curious and instructive side-lights upon the mind of the Church in the fourth century. As in the case of his doctrine of the Trinity and the person of Christ, it is not so much the orthodoxy or heterodoxy as the utter independence of Aphraates which strikes the modern reader. The good bishop goes on in his easy simple style with a tone of assured authority and unconsciousness of serious opposition, and it is only when we pause and try to fit his utterances into the schemes of doctrine and practice with which we are familiar that we realise that we are moving in another world. The Church of Aphraates, like the Church of S. Athanasius, is the legitimate child of second-century Christianity, but it has come by another line of descent and the cousins have not all things in common.

With regard to the Lord's Supper Aphraates is comparatively normal. In the Eucharist the faithful partake of the Body and Blood of Christ. It must be taken fasting, but the fast must be such as once for all was prescribed by Isaiah, "for always is fasting from evil things better than fasting from bread and water[1]." The fasting of Abel and Enoch, of innocent Noah, of faithful Abraham, of unrevengeful Joseph are to be our models. "If purity of heart be absent, the fast is not accepted. And remember and see, my beloved, that it is well that a man should cleanse his heart and keep his tongue and cleanse his hands of evil; for it is not fitting to mix honey and wormwood. For if a man would fast from bread and water, let him not mix with his fasting abuse and cursing. Thou hast but one door to thy house—that house which is a Temple of God; it doth not beseem thee, O man, that by the door where the King doth enter in

[1] III 8.

should come forth filth and dirt! For when a man will fast from all that is abominable and will take the Body and Blood of the Messiah, let him take heed to his mouth whereby the King doth enter in. Thou hast no right, O man, through that same mouth to give out unclean words! Hear what our Saviour saith : *That which entereth into a man doth not defile him; but that which cometh forth from the mouth, that defileth him* [1]." The fast here enjoined is metaphorical, but there can be no doubt that Aphraates teaches the doctrine that our Lord is physically present in the consecrated elements.

We may pause by the way to note Aphraates' singular and picturesque explanation of the three days and three nights among the dead which Christ had predicted for Himself. In his discourse on the Passover [2] he says that our Lord gave His Body and Blood to the disciples at the Last Supper. But, he argues, he whose body is eaten [3]

---

[1] III 2.   [2] XII 6, 7.

[3] In XII 9 (*Wright*, p. 222, line 3) we must read *'akil* : the MS. has *'ekal* (or *'âkêl*).

and blood drunk is already counted among the dead. The three days and three nights are to be reckoned from the time of the Supper, and, as Aphraates puts the three hours' darkness as one whole night and the ensuing time of light on Good Friday afternoon as one whole day, he has no difficulty in making up the required number. Moreover, he adds, this is why Christ kept silence before Pilate and the Jews, for it was impossible that one who is counted among the dead should speak.

These things, however, belong to the curiosities of exegesis: they do not have much bearing upon the general history of Christian Doctrine. It is otherwise with the theory of Baptism as presented to us in Discourse VII.

The majority of the references to Baptism in Aphraates contain little that is especially startling. Christian baptism is the true circumcision[1]; it is administered, as we have already seen, in the Names of the Three Persons of the Trinity[2]; by baptism

---

[1] XII 9. [2] XXIII 63: see above, p. 36.

regeneration is conferred, sins are washed away[1], and the body is preserved in the Day of Judgement[2]. "From baptism do we receive the Spirit of the Messiah. For in the same hour that the priests invoke the Spirit, the heavens open and it cometh down and broodeth upon the waters, and they that are baptized are clothed with it. For from all that are born of the body the Spirit is far away, until they come to the Birth by water, and then they receive the Holy Spirit[3]." In accordance with ancient custom the rite of baptism is performed at Easter[4].

All this is normal, regular, almost commonplace. Suddenly we are transported into a different planet. Baptism is not the common seal of every Christian's faith, but a privilege reserved for monks.

The passage where this amazing view is enforced is so important that I give it at length. In the Discourse upon Penitents, after reciting the story of Gideon who by the trial of water picked out his

---

[1] IV 19.   [2] VI 14.
[3] VI 14: cf. *Gwynn*, p. 371.   [4] XII 13.

three hundred from ten thousand men, and after quoting our Lord's words that many are called but few chosen, Aphraates goes on to say[1]: "Wherefore thus should the trumpeters, the heralds of the Church, cry and warn all the Society of God before the Baptism—them, I say, that have offered themselves for virginity and for holiness, youths and maidens holy—them shall the heralds warn. And they shall say : He whose heart is set to the state of matrimony, let him marry before baptism, lest he fall in the spiritual contest and be killed. And he that feareth this part of the struggle let him turn back, lest he break his brother's heart like his own. He also that loveth his possessions let him turn back from the army, lest when the battle shall wax too fierce for him he may remember his property and turn back, and he that turneth back then is covered with disgrace. He that hath not offered himself and hath not yet put on his armour, if he turn back he is not blamed ; but every one that doth offer himself and put on his armour, if he

[1] VII 20.

4—2

turn back from the contest becometh a laughing-stock."

This is a strange exhortation, strange at least to us Westerns. Perhaps it was not so much Constantine's fault as the fault of his spiritual advisers that his famous baptism was so long delayed. But indeed this deliberate reservation of baptism for the spiritual aristocracy of Christendom shews us that we are dealing with a view of the sacraments quite other than the Catholic view. Those who are not yet baptised may nevertheless, according to Aphraates, belong to the Society of God[1], and if they do not volunteer for the sacramental life they are not blamed.

I need scarcely remind you that Aphraates is not alone in holding this theory of the sacraments. It was the theory of the Marcionites, and we shall see that it was enforced with even greater rigour by the unorthodox party in the Syriac-speaking Church. Something like it also reappears in the Paulicians

---

[1] *Q'yâmeh dAlâhâ.*

and Cathars of a later day[1]. So also, I suppose, Buddhism is a community of monks : the people are adherents, not members of the body.

It is very difficult to pass a true judgement upon Aphraates' conception of the Christian life. So much depends on the amount of influence which the inner community had upon the mass of the people, or, looking at the matter from another point of view, how much the unbaptised lay Christian felt himself to be a member of Christ. Unfortunately we have very little evidence on these points.

One thing at least is certain. We who live in a sacramental system of Christianity, whether we be Catholics or Protestants, ought to be deeply grateful to the true instinct which produced the sacrament of Holy Matrimony. It is not by chance that Dom Parisot in his ingenious *Introduction* to the writings of Aphraates was unable to find any reference to this institution, for I suspect that our Persian Sage would have recoiled from the thought

[1] See especially the Cathar ritual in Mr Conybeare's *Key of Truth*, pp. 160—170.

of such a ceremony with horror. We are so accustomed to the solemnisation of weddings that we may easily come to think of the act as natural and inevitable, but the words of Aphraates teach us that it was not always so regarded. It is surely no light gain to Christian society that the bridal feast has been hallowed with the blessing of the Church.

With this we must take leave of Aphraates and the orthodox circles of the Syriac Church. I hope I have succeeded in leaving upon you a favourable impression of the Persian Sage. As a theologian, his modesty in speculation and his abstinence from abusive language are virtues rare in his own age and admirable in all ages, while his independent knowledge of the Bible has hardly been equalled among the Fathers[1]. As a writer and as a theologian he is greatly superior to his more famous contemporary S. Ephraim, the poverty of whose thought is scarcely more appalling than the fecundity of his pen.

---

[1] It must have required no small amount of courage, as well as intelligence, to reject the application of Lam iv 20 to Christ: cf. Just. *Ap.* I 55; Tert. *adv. Marc.* III 6, etc.

'BARDESANES' DE FATO.

THE philosophical dialogue known as 'Bardesanes *De Fato*' is not the work of Bardaisan himself but of his disciple Philip. It was composed not long after the Romans had taken possession of Edessa, *i.e.* about the middle of the 3rd century. In form it is modelled upon the Dialogues of Plato, Bardaisan taking the place of Socrates as the chief speaker and the teacher of a younger generation.

I do not now propose to enter upon any full discussion of the dialogue, not because it is not interesting in itself, but because the school out of which it came exercised only an indirect influence upon the later developments of the Syriac-speaking Church. The disciples of Bardaisan, like their great master, were tainted with heresy, and I imagine that the *De Fato* owes its preservation to what is but a side-interest, *viz.* the graphic descriptions contained in it of the varied customs of the nations of the earth with regard to marriage and other social observances. In fact, the title of the work in our MS. is 'The Book of the Laws of the Countries[1].'

The main object of the dialogue is to expound the doctrine of the three influences which are at work upon man. These are his *Nature*, his *Fate*, and his *Free-will*. By Nature men are born, they grow to maturity and age, and they die : so far all men are alike. By their Fate distinctions are introduced between them,—the distinctions of wealth and poverty, beauty and ugliness, health and sickness. These are not wholly in our power and come, at least partly, by Fate ; for the doctrine that misfortunes are all sent as punishments for sin is expressly rejected[2]. But in addition to their Nature and their Fate men are moved by their

[1] The dialogue was discovered by Cureton, and edited in his *Spicilegium Syriacum*, 1855.   [2] *Spicilegium*, p. 9.

Free-will, which has been given to them as a gift from God's bounty. It is in respect of this gift of Free-will that man was made in the image of God[1]. By his Free-will a man can modify his Fate to some extent, and with regard to his Free-will, and that alone, will he be judged at the Last Day. Moreover the commandments of God are such that they are easy, for they are independent of Fate, and only the Will is needed to perform them. Even if a man be poor and sick he can love and bless and speak the truth, and can pray for the good of every man he knows, while if he be rich and strong he can in addition help his neighbour. Nothing can hinder us from these things : we are not commanded to do anything involving bodily strength or mental cleverness. Nay more, when a man does well and abstains from evil he is glad—every man, that is, except those who were created not for good and are called tares[2]. The commandments of God are easy : it is success in this life that is barred with obstacles[3].

---

[1] *Spicilegium,* pp. 3, 4.   [2] *Ibid.* p. 5 *ad fin.*   [3] *Ibid.* p. 7.

The proof of the existence of Free-will in man is made to rest partly on the diversity of customs of various nations of men compared with the uniformity of each species of animal all over the world, and partly on the actual observed changes of human customs arising from royal decrees to conquered subjects or now in these last days from conversion to the new race of us Christians[1].

Two points in this curious and interesting work appear to me to deserve attention. The first is the strongly religious tone by which it is marked,—religious, that is, as distinct from ecclesiastical or merely speculative. The dialogue starts with the old question why God did not make man so that he should not sin, and the judgement to come is not taught but assumed. It is the fear of God which sets us free from all other fears[2]. At the same time the tone of the book is singularly unecclesiastical. The Unity of God and the Judgement are the only doctrines of the Church which present themselves, while but for a passing reference to the

[1] *Spicileg.*, p. 20.   [2] *Ibid.* p. 2.

Parable of the Sower we might have supposed that the author was ignorant of the New Testament. But the almost Jewish tone of parts of the dialogue is of more than passing interest, when we remember the Jewish culture of Aphraates[1]. Though the form of the dialogue is borrowed from Plato, the spirit is Semitic : the hands may be the hands of Esau, but the voice is the voice of Jacob.

The other point which I wish to notice here is the very curious doctrine of the composition of the Cosmos, a doctrine certainly rare in Christian writings and perhaps due to Bardaisan himself. According to this doctrine the Universe is compounded of what the author calls *Îthyê* or Elemental Beings. These, if not eternal, were at least pre-existent to the present order of things, and the work of creation consisted above all in arranging the Elements out of Chaos into an Order, whereby the Elements could neither do serious injury to

[1] Note that in Gen i 26 the dialogue says man was made ' in the image of *Elohim*,' not simply ' in the image of God ': cf. Gen vi 1 *Pesh.*

each other nor be seriously injured themselves. The Machine has been set going, and the Parts do not collide, as they would if they had been left to themselves and their spheres of action not strictly limited. Nevertheless even the Elements have some degree of freedom, and for this they also will appear to be judged at the Last Day. But their freedom is but small compared with that of man's : it is in respect to his freedom that man stands at the head of creation[1].

It is a picturesque conception. According to Bardaisan the world was not brought into being out of nothing, nor formed of matter naturally inert, but it is a beautifully balanced combination of independent and often antagonistic forces. I do not think we shall do justice to the fundamental idea unless for the Sun and the Moon, the Sea and the Winds, we substitute in thought the forces of nature which make up our modern universe, such properties of matter I mean as Gravitation and Electricity.

[1] *Spicileg.*, pp. 4, 21.

But after our excursion into the fascinating wilderness of cosmic speculation we must not forget that the same theory of man's place in the universe has already met us in Aphraates. After reading the dialogue *De Fato* it does not come to us with such a shock to hear the argument of Aphraates that God Almighty has not denied the name of God and of Son to men, though He has expressly forbidden such an honour to be given to the Sun and the Moon and the host of Heaven[1].

I must pass by the bright star of all Syriac literature, the great Hymn of the Soul that went down to Egypt for the One Pearl. This, the most noble poem of Christian Antiquity, is no doubt familiar to all of you: it is worth while to learn Syriac, so as to be able to read it in the original. All I need point out here is that the same conceptions of the Trinity—perhaps I ought rather to say, the same metaphors for the relations of the

[1] See above, p. 42.

Trinity to man—are found in the Hymn as in other early Syriac literature. The *King of Kings*, the *Queen of the East*, and the *Viceroy*, the next in rank, are respectively the Father, Mother and Brother of the Soul : there can be little doubt that they correspond to the Father, the Holy Spirit, and the Son.

THE ACTS OF JUDAS THOMAS.

WE have now come to that original and characteristic product of early Syriac-speaking Christianity,
the *Acts* of Judas Thomas, the brother of our Lord
and the Apostle of India.

I am quite aware that this statement is highly
controversial. The *Acta Thomae* are commonly
supposed to be one of a series of fabulous Greek
tales describing the missionary adventures of all the
Apostles. This conception of the work I hold to
be altogether erroneous. That the stories told in
the *Acts of Thomas* have little or no historical basis
is indeed almost self-evident, but I do not believe
that it was intended to form part of a series, and
I believe most firmly that it was originally composed
in Syriac, not Greek. Possibly also I ought to

defend myself for investing an admittedly fabulous narrative with so much importance. It is not so very long ago since students of Church history might be divided into the credulous folk who wholly or partly believed these tales, and the wise who neglected them altogether. But the present generation is too much accustomed to the serious religious novel not to be in sympathy with a doctrinal work cast in narrative form. That the *Acts of Thomas* is the work of a man very much in earnest there can be no manner of doubt. The style is simple, as becomes the narrative setting, but it is as truly a book of religious philosophy as the *Pilgrim's Progress*, and it demands from us serious study.

Before indicating the main grounds upon which I regard these Acts as a Syriac work it may be not superfluous to give a short abstract of the story which forms the framework of the book[1].

I. At the beginning we are told how the

[1] A complete English Translation is given in Wright's *Apocryphal Acts*, vol. ii, pp. 146—298.

Twelve Apostles divided the countries of the earth among themselves by lot, and that the lot which fell to Judas Thomas—Judas the Twin—was India. But Judas Thomas did not wish to go and preach to the Indians, so our Lord appeared to an Indian merchant named Ḥabbân, a servant of King Gundaphar, and sold Thomas to him as a slave. Thomas and Ḥabbân go off by sea and disembark at the town of Sandarûk (*or*, Sanadrûk). Here they find that the King of the place is making a great feast to celebrate his only daughter's marriage, and they go in with the rest to the feast. At the feast Thomas sings a curious Hymn : he also prophesies the violent death of one of the guests, an event which comes to pass that very night. The King hears of this and forces Thomas to go in and pray over the bride. He does so and then departs. But when the bride and bridegroom are alone our Lord Himself appears to them in the likeness of Thomas and persuades them both to a life of virginity. In the end the King also is converted, and the young people join St Thomas in India.

B.   5

II.　Meanwhile Thomas and Ḥabbân had gone on to King Gundaphar in India, and Thomas agrees to build a palace for the King. But all the money that is given him for the palace he spends among the poor. When King Gundaphar discovers it he is very angry, and casts Thomas into prison till he shall make up his mind by what death he shall die. Now that very night Gad, the King's brother, dies and is taken by angels to heaven : there he sees a magnificent palace, which is the very palace that has been built for his brother by the Apostle. So Gad begs to be allowed to come back to life that he may buy the palace from the King, as he does not know its value. This is granted ; but when the King hears the tale he understands and believes. Thomas is set free, and the King and his brother are both baptised in a bath-house and receive the Eucharist.

III.　After this Judas Thomas brings to life a youth who had been killed by a devil in the form of a black snake[1].

[1] In this story, as in some of the others, the prayers and exhortations of Thomas are given at considerable length.

IV. Next an ass's colt, of the stock that served Balaam the prophet, comes and speaks and directs Thomas to the city. At the gate of the city the colt falls down and dies, having performed its mission.

V. In the city Thomas delivers a beautiful woman from the attacks of a devil. The woman is baptised and she receives the Communion.

VI. During the ceremony a young man's hand withers, and he confesses that he had killed a woman who would not live a life of virginity with him. On his repentance he brings Judas Thomas to the dead woman's body, and by means of the Apostle she is brought to life again. She then describes the torments of the unchaste that she had seen in hell, and the episode closes with an exhortation.

VII. After these things while the Apostle is preaching in India, the General of King Mazdai comes beseeching him to free his wife and daughter from evil and lascivious devils. Judas Thomas leaves his converts under the care of the deacon

Xanthippus (*or*, Xenophon) and goes with the General. On the way the horses of their chariot break down, but four wild asses come to be harnessed in their stead, and with their help the devils are driven out and the women healed.

VIII. Soon after this a noble lady, by name Mygdonia, the wife of Cyrus[1], a kinsman of King Mazdai, is converted by Thomas to the life of virginity. Cyrus is in despair; and when his personal influence fails to move Mygdonia, he goes and complains to the King, who sends and arrests Thomas at the house of Ṣîfûr the General. Thomas is scourged and sent to prison, where he sings a Hymn of praise[2]. But Mygdonia remains firm, and secretly visits Thomas in the prison with her nurse Narqia : there he baptises them and celebrates the Eucharist. In the meanwhile King Mazdai

---

[1] The name Cyrus, in Syriac *Kôrêsh*, is preserved uncorrupted in the Sachau MS. In the British Museum MS. it is misspelt *Kârîsh*, and in the Greek corrupted to Χαρίσιος.

[2] In front of this Hymn, which is undoubtedly a genuine portion of the *Acts*, the British Museum Codex inserts the great Hymn of the Soul.

and Cyrus, who regard the conversion of Mygdonia as due to magic and enchantment, agree to let Thomas go if he will tell her to be as she was before. Thomas warns them that it will be useless, and that neither his persuasion nor tortures would change her new spirit : this is proved to be the case, and Mygdonia refuses to listen to the Apostle when he pretends to tell her to go back to her husband. After this Thomas returns to the house of Ṣîfûr the General and baptises him and his family, and gives them also the Eucharist : at the same time Mygdonia converts Tertia, the wife of King Mazdai. Mazdai now becomes seriously angry and drags Thomas off to prison again, but on the way he converts Vîzân, the King's son. In the prison the Apostle makes his final address, beginning with the Lord's Prayer. Manashar, Vîzân's wife (who has just been healed of a long sickness by our Lord Himself appearing to her in the form of a youth), joins them in the prison, and the Apostle baptises Vîzân, Manashar, and Tertia. In the morning Thomas is brought out and condemned to death by

the King: he is taken outside the town and after a
short prayer is speared by four soldiers. Before his
death he ordains Ṣîfûr and Vîzân, and the converts
continue in the faith after being encouraged by a
vision of the ascended Judas Thomas.

The bones of the Apostle were secretly taken
away to the 'West' by one of the brethren, but a
long time afterwards the dust from the grave charms
away a devil from one of King Mazdai's sons,
whereupon the king also believes and prays Ṣîfûr
and the brethren for forgiveness.

Such is the tale of St Thomas. It is quite
possible that some of the details of the legend are
older than our *Acts*. The reputed bones of the
Apostle were preserved at Edessa, and doubtless
some story of their adventures had grown up around
the shrine. But the real interest of the *Acts* is not
historical, any more than the interest of *Lear* or
Hamlet is historical. The interest lies in the
prayers and sermons of Judas Thomas. These are
not mere embellishments of the narrative, but the

very essence of the book. What the author wishes us to give our earnest attention to is the Gospel of Virginity and Poverty and its effect upon the soul. As to the intense seriousness of the book there can be no doubt at all : no early Christian writer, orthodox or heterodox, would quote the Lord's Prayer in full merely for ornament.

It will be noticed even from this short summary that the *Acts of Thomas* form a work complete in itself. From the moment that St Thomas starts for India we hear no more of the other Apostles. He is absolutely independent of every one except his Lord. The word Church occurs only once and that by mistake[1]. Moreover the whole framework of the tale is Eastern, and Eastern of a very decided type. The proper names are such as would occur to a Syriac-speaking Christian, but they could hardly have been invented by a Greek. It is to Justi's *Iranisches Namenbuch* not to Pape's *Griechische Eigennamen* that we have to look for their

---

[1] The first word of the *Hymn* in the first Act: the Greek has ἡ κόρη.

elucidation. Cyrus—not in the Greek but in an approximation to the genuine Oriental form— Mazdai, Vîzân, Manashar, are good old Persian names. Mygdonia is another name for Nisibis. Except Xenophon the deacon and Tertia the queen there is not one European-sounding name among them.

But the main argument for regarding the *Acta Thomae* as an original Syriac composition is independent of these general considerations. It consists in the large number of passages where the existing Greek is either a mistranslation or a misreading of the Syriac. The Greek and the Syriac often diverge freely from one another, and there is often no attempt to translate literally ; but in a sufficient number of instances the evidence is clear enough for an induction.

A full critical discussion involves considerations of Syriac grammar and palaeography and would be out of place here : I must refer the reader to my paper in the *Journal of Theological Studies* for October, 1899. At the same time I will indicate in a couple of examples the nature of the evidence.

When Judas Thomas is about to go away with Ṣifûr the General to cure his wife and daughter he bids farewell to his converts, and says to them : "Be ye holding to us and looking at us as the ministers of God ; though we also, if we do not *take pains* that we may be worthy of this name, *punishment* we shall receive, and for judgment and requital it will be to us" (Wright, *Syriac Text* 237[11–14] = Bonnet, *Acta Thomae* 48[13–16]).   The corresponding Greek has : "Remember us, as also we remember you : for unless we *fulfil the burden of the commandments* (τὸ τῶν ἐντολῶν φορτίον τελέσωμεν) we shall not be worthy heralds of the name of Christ, and moreover shall receive at the last *punishment for our own heads* (τὴν τιμωρίαν ... τῆς ἑαυτῶν κεφαλῆς)".   Here there is wide divergence, but a glance at the Syriac at once reveals its origin.   The Syriac idiom for 'to take pains' is literally 'to take up the burden' and a word-for-word rendering of the Syriac in this passage would be " if we do not take up the burden that we may be worthy of this name." The Greek translator misunderstood the phrase, and in his version he brought in the wholly foreign conception of submitting to the yoke of the law. Similarly, the odd introduction of κεφαλή in the latter part of the sentence comes from the fact that the Syriac word for punishment (not necessarily capital) is literally " a putting on the head." It would be a miracle indeed if the Greek were original here and the Syriac with its characteristic and perfectly natural idioms a translation.

One example more. You will remember that the daughter of the King of Sandarûk was converted with her husband to a life of Christian virginity on her bridal night. The next morning her mother expostulates with her. In the girl's reply she says among other things, according to the Greek (*Bonnet* 12¹⁹), ἐξουθένισα τὸν ἄνδρα τοῦτον *I have despised this man*, i.e. her husband. This is, to say the least, surprising. The young man had just been converted along with herself, and to despise one's fellow-believers has never been a Christian virtue, even in the most heretical sects.   But the difficulty vanishes when we look at the Syriac, which has not 'this *man*' but 'this *deed*,' i.e. the ἔργον τῆς αἰσχύνης mentioned three lines before[1].   In Syriac writing *gaβrâ* 'man' and *"βâδâ* 'deed' are almost exactly alike, different as they sound.   Thus the unsatisfactory expression in the Greek is easily explicable as a translator's misreading : on any other hypothesis it would be difficult to account for its presence.

These are but two instances out of many, and in what follows I shall feel justified in assuming the *Acts of Thomas* to be an original Syriac composition. I need only add that the same view is held by Nöldeke, and (as I have learnt quite lately) it was also maintained by the late Prof. R. L. Bensly.

But if these *Acts* be of Syriac origin we are dealing with a work immensely important for the history of Christian thought in the Euphrates Valley. To begin with, the work is one of the oldest non-biblical monuments of Syriac literature.   The text

[1] Cf. also *Wright* 299[20].

of the quotations from the Gospels alone would be enough to shew this. Whatever editorial touches the *Acts of Thomas* may have received, the Scripture allusions have been left in their original form, for they follow the Old Syriac, not the Peshitta. Notably this is the case with the Lord's Prayer, which as I remarked above is quoted in full, and in agreement with the very striking renderings of Cureton's text. The example of Aphraates warns us, it is true, from dating a Syriac work early because its doctrinal statements appear too primitive for the 4th century, but in the case of the *Acts of Thomas* we have to take into account the popularity of the book even in orthodox circles. There are clear references to it in Ephraim[1], and Jacob of Serug wrote a poem on the Palace which St Thomas built in Heaven for the King of India. I do not think we shall be far wrong if we put the date of our *Acts* before the middle of the 3rd century. Of course they have suffered a little in transmission. Here and there a too definitely unorthodox clause has

[1] *Carm. Nisib.* 42.

been excised altogether or some harmless platitude has been substituted, but the general accuracy of the text as published by Wright is attested by the very ancient palimpsest fragments at Sinai.

I have designated the work as unorthodox. This perhaps requires some justification. Judged by an Athanasian standard it is of course quite heretical, but the standard of the early Syriac-speaking Churches was nearer that of Aphraates. To my own mind the un-catholic note is struck in the puritan recklessness of the writer: he never allows for the weakness of humanity or for the economy of Church government. This is the note of Tertullian, of Montanus, of the Donatists—the note struck in our own century by Edward Irving. But more definite indications are not wanting. In the first place, I cannot believe that an orthodox circle would have developed the very remarkable belief that Judas Thomas—Judas the Twin—was the twin-brother of our Lord Himself. Not only do men and women in these *Acts* mistake the one for the other, but the very devils and wild beasts salute the Apostle as ' Twin of the Messiah[1].'   No wonder that some of the MSS. have obliterated this title !

The argument commonly relied upon for regarding the *Acta Thomae* as 'Gnostic' is the occurrence of certain mystical and very imperfectly understood expressions in the prayers and invocations.   Some few of these have disappeared in Syriac from the text as preserved in the British Museum MS. used by Wright, and many more have been left out in the Sachau MS. at Berlin : but in some cases at least the queer phrases in the Greek are the result not of heterodox doctrine but of the ignorance or helplessness of the writer[2].   The discussion of such points involves critical details and the niceties of Semitic grammar : all that needs to be pointed out here is the improbability that a writer so much in earnest as the author of the *Acts* would indicate an elaborate and strange cosmogony by a few side touches.

[1] *Wright* 197, 208.
[2] *E.g. Bonnet* 30[11-13] (= *Wright* 209[10-13]): cf. Gen i 2 *in the Peshitta.*

In any case there is a great gulf fixed between these *Acts* and the thoroughly Greek Gnostic *Acts of John*. According to the *Acts of John* the highest gift of the true Christian is spiritual insight to perceive the hidden meaning of that which is hidden from the uninstructed believer. "Behold Me," Christ says there to St John, "in truth that I am, not what I said, but what thou art able to know.... The things that they say of Me I had not, and the things that they say not those I suffered. Now what they are I will signify unto thee, for I know that thou wilt understand[1]." The language of the *Acts of Judas Thomas* is quite other than this. Not philosophy but ethics is here the essence of Christianity : the chief aim of the writer is to produce a change of conduct, not spiritual enlightenment. St Thomas knows that the mysteries of life cannot be rightly uttered in human speech, but so far as may be he expounds them to all the people. There is no intentional concealment of doctrine, no inner circle of *Illuminati*.

[1] *Acta Iohannis* XV (James, *Apocrypha Anecdota* ii, p. 20 ff.).

These *Acts* strike a higher, shriller, note than that of Catholicism, but now and again it rings true. If we overlook the fantastic machinery of the tale, and remember that the author was living in a world distracted by the indecisive yet devastating struggle of Greek and Persian, a world also where what there was of art, of science, of philosophy, was still wholly pagan, we shall find something with which to sympathise and even something to inspire. No one, save only St Francis of Assisi, has ever so whole-heartedly preached in the spirit of the Sermon on the Mount. Nowhere in Christian literature do the merchant's goods appear so little in comparison with the Pearl of great price. "As long as we are in the world," says St Thomas, "we are unable to speak about that which all the believers in God are going to receive. For if we say that He hath given us Light, we mention something which we have seen ; and if we say that He hath given us Wealth, we mention something that is in the world ; and if we speak of Clothing, we mention something that nobles wear; and if we speak of dainty Meats, we mention something against which we are warned; and if we speak of this temporary Rest, a chastisement is appointed for it. But we speak of God and of our Lord Jesus, and of Angels and Watchers and Holy Ones, and of the New World, and of the incorruptible food of the tree of Life, and of the draught of the water of Life; of what Eye hath not seen, nor Ear heard, nor hath it entered into the Heart of man to conceive,—what God hath prepared from of old for those who love him[1]." Surely this is the language of Gnosticism at its best. It is unencumbered with irrelevant details about the origin and physical constitution of the universe, it is couched in no uncouth jargon of Æons and Emanations, but it expresses as clearly as words can speak the great doctrine that our knowledge and our terminology is and must always remain relative and approximate. All things are said in Figures, because the Things Eternal are the things that are not seen, neither can they be named with a name.

[1] *Wright* 205; Eng. Tr. 177.

B.   6

The teaching of the *Acts of Thomas* contains
another feature which must not remain unnoticed.
It is a feature which, though not heretical in itself,
is in early documents characteristic rather of Gnostic
thought than of Catholic teaching. This is the
lack of interest in controversy against the Jews and
against idolatry. Judas Thomas does not bring
forward unorthodox opinions about the old dispen-
sation or the worship of heathen gods : he simply
passes these things by with the turn of a phrase.
Thus we read (Transl. p. 207) that God's will was
spoken by the Prophets, but Israel did not obey
because of their evil genius[1]. Again, the devils
confess that they take pleasure in sacrifices and
libations of wine on the altars as well as in murder
and adultery (Transl. p. 213)[2]. But these are
mere allusions by the way : it is not so much
against the gods that St Thomas preaches as against
the evil nature in man. Contrast this with the

---

[1] In the Syriac, *yaṣr'hôn bîshâ*: cf. Deut xxxi 21 and the
corresponding Jewish doctrines.

[2] See also Transl. p. 198.

elaborate polemic against the Jews in Aphraates, and the long sermons against idolatry in the *Doctrine of Addai*. So much indeed is it the rule that the 'Acts' of martyrs should contain a testimony against the worship of idols that in the Latin version of the *Acta Thomae* there is an extended interpolation, telling how St Thomas refused to worship the Sun-god when he was brought before King Mazdai.

The interest of the author of the *Acts of Thomas* lay in the workings of human nature, not in the conflicting claims of rival religions—in a word, it lay in the conversion of individual souls rather than in the establishment of a Church. But to the Catholic writers from the very earliest period the case was different. To them the Jewish question was vital, not so much for the sake of convincing the Jews of error as to establish their own position. There stood the Holy Oracles, the promises of God to His people—to whom did they apply? It was as essential for the early Church to establish her claim to be the true heir of the Covenants, as

6—2

it is for the High Anglican of our day to make out a case for the apostolical succession of the English bishops. With the Gnostics, unless I am mistaken, the position of things was not quite the same. Early Catholicism was a historical religion, proved by texts out of the Old Testament and by the events of the life of Jesus of Nazareth : Gnosticism, on the other hand, was what we call natural religion, a philosophy. The philosophy might be illustrated from the Old Testament or the New, but it was really independent of the Bible. It was not the application of the old promises of God that troubled the author of the *Acts of Thomas* but the aimlessness of men's lives, which to him appeared to be filled with care and sorrow about that which must quickly pass away for ever.

In the conception of the Church—that is, the organised body of believers,—as a thing in itself to be worked for and fostered, lies, I think, the point of difference between Catholicism and Gnosticism, between Aphraates and the *Acts of Thomas*. To the convert of Judas Thomas there was literally

nothing left on this earth to live for. "Would
that the days passed swiftly over me, and that all
the hours were one," says Mygdonia, "that I
might go forth from this world, and go and see
that Beautiful One with whose impress I have been
sealed[1], that Living One and Giver of life to those
who have believed in Him, where there is neither
day nor night, and no darkness but light, and
neither good nor bad, nor rich nor poor, neither
male nor female, nor slaves nor freemen, nor any
proud and uplifted over those who are humble[2]."
The old civilisation was doomed, but this religious
Nihilism puts nothing in its place. To the orthodox
Christian, on the other hand, the Church stood as a
middle term between the things of the next world
and of this. It was the Body of Christ and
therefore eternal; something worth living for and
working for. Yet it was in the world as much as
the Empire itself. The idea of the Church thus

---

[1] *I.e.* 'into whose Name I have been baptised.' Wright's text
must here be corrected from the Sachau MS.

[2] *Wright*, Transl. p. 265.

formed an invaluable fixed point, round which a new civilisation could slowly crystallise.

But to return to our main subject. The chief characteristics, the chief *differentia*, of early Christianity outside the Roman Empire in the only region where it is to be found, have their origin either in the ascetic ideal or in the absence of the specifically Greek philosophical influence. Now for reasons very unlike these two points should have a great interest to us English-speaking Christians. Instead of sitting in judgment, therefore, upon the shortcomings of the ancient Church of the Euphrates Valley and pointing out its unsuitableness for the age of Constantine and the requirements of the Byzantine Empire, I wish to recommend the early history and doctrines of that Church to your study and your sympathy. We also have no part nor lot in the Empire, and our philosophy is not in bondage to the Greeks. Upon us will come, sooner or later, the task of adjusting our Faith and our Science, of reconciling the Catholic Religion with Christian Verity, as the Athanasian Creed puts it. In the Christian Verity—that is, Theological Science,—of the 4th century there was much that was temporary, ignorant, Greek, as indeed there is in the science, Christian or otherwise, of our own day. I think it will help not only the historical investigator of the history of dogma, but also those who are fashioning the channel of our own beliefs to take serious account of the non-Greek Church of the East.

The spirit of Asceticism touches us from another side. In these cold climates the ascetic ideal has never been a really dominant factor. It is always necessary to make so much provision for the flesh that it is impossible to aim at forgetting its requirements. Even at Marseilles, in Cassian's day, it provoked merely ridicule when some of the monks attempted to live as the Egyptians lived in the warm, dry deserts. But the British Empire covers many lands and many climates, and it is the simple fact that in the land where Judas Thomas is fabled to have lived and taught the natural instincts of the

people still identify true religion with the life of the
wandering mendicant. The other day a lady,
the wife of a missionary who has spent many
years with her husband at a mission station in
Southern India, told me that when Christianity
really takes possession of a native of India, when he
becomes really converted, he is frequently anxious
to take up the wandering ascetic life. I shewed
my friend the *Acts of Judas Thomas*, and she was
interested to find in it so much of the ethical type
which an Indian convert would naturally be disposed
to admire. These converts, remember, are Protestants who have heard of Christianity only through
the stately and respectable formularies of the
Church of England or through one of the sects
of English nonconformists. *O testimonium animae
naturaliter—asceticae!* But if asceticism grows so
naturally and inevitably on Eastern soil it must be
a fact of human nature with which we have to
reckon—to direct and educate, it may be, but not
altogether to repress. Even if the heathen 'ascetic'
of modern India has often more points in common

with the Friar of the later middle ages than with St Francis of Assisi or Judas Thomas, yet he represents an ideal not wholly alien to the teaching of the New Testament. We live in an age of a victorious and progressive material civilisation: even if we are content to enter into life by keeping the commandments only, it may be well to remember the counsel of perfection which our Lord Himself gave to the rich young man. To refuse to listen to the note struck so eloquently, if so monotonously, in the *Acts of Judas Thomas* is to neglect one of the features which distinguish men from the beasts that perish.

CONTENTS.

GORGIAS REPRINT SERIES

1. J. B. Segal, *Edessa 'The Blessed City'* (2001, based on the 1970 edition).
2. J. Hamlyn Hill, *The Earliest Life of Christ: The Diatessaron of Tatian* (2001, based on the 1910 2nd abridged edition).
3. Joseph Knanishu, *About Persia and Its People* (2001, based on the 1899 edition).
4. Robert Curzon, *Ancient Monasteries of the East, Or The Monasteries of the Levant* (2001, based on the 1849 edition).
5. William Wright, *A Short History of Syriac Literature* (2001, based on the 1894 edition).
6. Frits Holm, *My Nestorian Adventure in China, A Popular Account of the Holm-Nestorian Expedition to Sian-Fu and Its Results* (2001, based on the 1924 edition).
7. Austen Henry Layard, *Nineveh and Its Remains: an account of a visit to the Chaldean Christians of Kurdistan, and the Yezidis, or devil-worshipers; and an inquiry into the manners and arts of the ancient Assyrians*, Vol. 1 (2001, based on the 1850 5th edition).
8. Austen Henry Layard, *Nineveh and Its Remains*, Vol. 2 (2001, based on the 1850 5th edition).
9. Margaret Gibson, *How the Codex Was Found, A Narrative of Two Visits to Sinai From Mrs. Lewis's Journals 1892-1893* (2001, based on the 1893 edition).
10. Richard Davey, *The Sultan and His Subjects* (2001, based on the 1907 edition).
11. Adrian Fortescue, *Eastern Churches Trilogy: The Orthodox Eastern Church* (2001, based on the 1929 edition).
12. Adrian Fortescue, *Eastern Churches Trilogy: The Lesser*

Eastern Churches (2001, based on the 1913 edition).

13. Adrian Fortescue, *Eastern Churches Trilogy: The Uniate Eastern Churches: the Byzantine Rite in Italy, Sicily, Syria and Egypt* (2001, based on the 1923 edition).

14. A. V. Williams Jackson, *From Constantinople to the Home of Omar Khayyam: Travels in Transcaucasia and Northern Persia for Historic and Literary Research* (2001, based on the 1911 edition).

15. Demetra Vaka, *The Unveiled Ladies of Stamboul* (2001, based on the 1923 edition).

16. Oswald H. Parry, *Six Months in a Syrian Monastery: Being the Record of a Visit to the Head Quarters of the Syrian Church in Mesopotamia with Some Account of the Yazidis or Devil Worshipers of Mosul and El Jilwah, Their Sacred Book* (2001, based on the 1895 edition).

17. B. T. A. Evetts, *The Churches and Monasteries of Egypt and Some Neighbouring Countries, Attribted to Abû Sâlih the Armenian* (2001, based on the 1895 edition).

18. James Murdock, *The New Testament, Or the Book of the Holy Gospel of Our Lord and Our God Jesus the Messiah, A Literal Translation from the Syriac Peshita Version* (2001, based on the 1851 edition).

19. Gertrude Lowthian Bell, *Amurath to Amurath: A Five Month Journey Along the Banks of the Euphrates* (2001, based on the 1924 second edition).

20. Smith, George. *Assyrian Discoveries: An Account of Explorations and Discoveries on the Site of Nineveh, During 1873 and 1874* (2002, based on the 1876 edition).

21. Dalley, Stephanie. *Mari and Karana, Two Old Babylonian Cities* (2002, first US paperback edition).

22. Grant, Asahel. *The Nestorians or the Lost Tribe* (2002, based on the 1841 edition).

23. O'Leary, De Lacy. *The Syriac Church and Fathers* (2002, based on the 1909 edition).

24. Burkitt, F. C. *Early Christianity Outside the Roman Empire* (2002, based on the 1909 edition).

25. Wigram, W. A. *The Assyrians and Their Neighbours*

(2002, based on the 1929 edition).

26. Kiraz, George. *Lexical Tools to the Syriac New Testament* (2002, first US edition).
27. Margoliouth, G. *Descriptive List of Syriac and Karshuni Manuscripts in the British Museum Acquired Since 1873* (2002, based on the 1899 edition).

Printed in the United States
72071LV00002B/39